The Poems of

© Copyright, Steven William Elliott, 2021.

All original works written and published by Steven William Elliott.

Stage name - Kapo.

All rights reserved.

MORE THAN A MIRACLE

She, the face I cannot see
Voice I cannot hear
Body I can't touch,
Maybe I love too much.
She's more than a miracle to me.

She, brings me round
Sings without sound
Born on a different cloud.
Quiet yet loud
She's more than a miracle to me.

Collect her footsteps, heal any bruise,
No worry, positivity to choose,
The sooner the better we admit good news,
Two hearts shine free.
She's more than a miracle to me.

Ignore those who are through,
Due to being blue.
Fearless giving is living,
Two branches, one tree.
She's more than a miracle to me.

Lost until I held her
Blind until I felt her,
I never knew dreams were free.
She's more than a miracle to me.

THE PROCESS

If your mind is on tomorrow's affairs
Today may suffer.
Pursuing potential repairs
Making today's troubles tougher.

Pain can pass to make life clear
To see and do.
But to live dreams, we must admit
There are nightmares to go through.

Today doesn't change length
Or place in the week.
You form purpose
Utilise times technique!

Can you recognise vocation
The flair of being free
If you haven't tasted contrast
Or felt your heart as an absentee.

No fret, no fear
'The process', be natural, be good!
Wisdom will hear
Chaos understood!

BUILD YOUR HEART A HOME

If your mind is in a storm,
Vision lost, all alone.
No ring on your telephone,
I will build your heart a home.

If the same four walls turn you cold,
Going backwards as you're growing old.
Tired of doing what you're told,
I will build your heart a home.

If silence tells you to run away,
But head reminds heart to stay,
I have a bed here where you can lay.
I will build your heart a home.

Cure all that gets you down,
Your heart of gold will soon be found,
Hands speaking, no sound,
I will build your heart a home.

I´ll cradle your life if you cultivate mine,
Sprinkle love until the end of time.
Everything fine; infinite reasons to shine,
I will build your heart a home.

RUST

She said she never wanted children
But I knew that she did.
Her gift to be a mother
Organically splendid.
Eyes of jewels,
Heart more golden than her hair.
The kind of angel a man is proud to take anywhere.

She had pains and concerns,
Deep menstrual burns
Reasons all valid and wise.
A romantic heart
Neglected from the start
Excuses to theorise lies.

Who can blame her soul?
Content, untouched
I could see when she blushed
The idea of children wasn't entirely flushed.
Instead a journey,
Yet to be made with a man unfound.

Head versus heart,
Womb versus trust
A science, a thrust
A choice she knows
That is neither a need nor must.
Reproduction or rust?

THE EVERLASTING

Don't prolong pain if wounded,
Don't drown in the past,
Let go of loves that no longer last.
Tears turn to wisdom,
Wisdom brings faith,
Faith in the everlasting love of life.

When life is hurtful
If nature misplaced her will
When you thought you grabbed it back
But you're still sliding downhill.
Feet find strength
Strength brings faith,
Faith in the everlasting love of life.

Let love carry you on
If you're lost in a storm
Or a hurricane of grief and deceit.
When you've escaped the whirlwind,
Clean face,
May eyes bring vision
Vision bring faith,
Faith in the everlasting love of life.

CHARIOT OF LOVE

Be the evening,
Scents free and blue
Twilight sky wealthy, inner being healthy,
Dreams there to pursue.

But my heart sank in time
No longer hear, feel or see
Visions of my first love
Singing in rhyme before me.

One day
Words brought me round.
A letter from my love,
Restoring magic, we had found.

'All the promises, words
And whispers I kissed to you,
Still ring true.
But the tears I caused
Can't be ignored,
It was me that felt the pain too,
It was me that was tangled in blue.
Trees and skies were far from my eyes
Vision slightly array.
But a voice from above
Gave me a choice
To ride in the Chariot of Love. '

ALLOW THE PAST

Allow the past to flicker and fade
If undivine inputs have overstayed.
Intrusions, welcome or not
Banish their aims, arms, and plot.

Bury it beneath sand or sea
You perceive, you´re the referee.
Execute with holy blade,
Delete, erase, trouble it's made.

Exhale the past, watch it flee
All disappeared, no debris.
Almost as if it was never there:
Not one sad memory, not even despair.

THOSE EYES THAT ARE JUST FOR ME

If only you could see them?
Those eyes that are just for me.
They hide behind big glasses you see,
Make her eyes appear bigger,
But they aren't her eyes.

I've seen her eyes up close
I've never seen jewels of the soul shine so bright.
Never seen a shy, loving, little girl
Hiding behind such a tall, brave, beautiful woman.

In her glasses, she acts tough
She's got to keep strong.
She's got to look strong.
But when I remove the glasses
I see her fully,
If only you could see them
Those eyes that are just for me.

THE GOLDFINCH

Blazing wings of gold
Drive through an air of calm.
Music bursting from a beating breast,
Reciting hymn, song and psalm.

A gliding flame heating the coast,
Building himself a nest.
Twig by twig, worm by worm,
A fortress built then blessed.

Guests from quests afar,
Admire the feathered orange chrome.
A crowned prophet of the sun
A globe to call his home.

Within his home the goldfinch will roam,
High then wide over land and sea.
Revealing himself from time to time,
Rejoicing as nature's definition of free.

ODE TO DOCTORS

Doctor oh doctor
One of love,
One of people, arts and friends
Carer for the community who tends
To tell a tale from travels.
As their story unravels
We learn they're one of a kind,
A humanist you will find.
A walking trophy of academia,
But they don't believe the hysteria
Instead they keep it real.
Face to face, there to assist,
From place to place, frequently missed
By lovers, family and friends.
They share a little wisdom,
Sprinkle a hint of charm
Never does harm,
A Peaceful Firearm.

Away from student days
Let's watch the different ways
They go about the game.
Already changed many lives and made many smiles
Yet so many more to come,
This world is ready for them.

THE MERMAID

As I searched for my soul
Amongst this sea of fish,
I encountered a mermaid
Who restored my faith.
She glittered through water,
Reflecting rays of love to all fins that passed by.
Then she approached,
Held me in her silk arms
And sang:

"Dear boy, what brings you here?
What are you seeking?
Your soul, you say? And fire?
Don't look too far or you could lose it.
Don't search too near as that may bring fear.
View yourself without thinking,
Then you´ll hear the birds singing,
Vibrantly, loud and clear."

I clenched a scroll from her,
She glared and sang:

'Use wisely dear child,
Don´t forget or confuse.
For labour and for duty,
Share righteous news!'

I entered a courthouse,
Sharing knowledge, fresh and new.
They sentenced me to stupidity,
Wisdom wasn't true.

I told Mr Military there is another way,
Killing is nonsense, there's nothing more to say.
He pressed a barrel against my head and yelled:
"Boy, flee town!
You will end my war,
Make me bankrupt,
With mere words and sound."

Rain fell, democrats brawled.
I wandered with the mermaid in mind.
I was glad she came to me.
I will send the message.
I will make us free.

-

County Kent, county Kent
Bumble bees of May.
County Kent, county Kent
Sweet honey and hay.

County Kent, county Kent
Breathe the pollen of June.
County Kent, county Kent
England's eastern moon.

FOR UTOPIA

Hearts rule hands, hands mould world.
Shared globe we admire, trot,
Same land where we hunt, plot,
How have so many forgot?

Forgot that air, water, wind and womb
Are necessities for the journey from cot to tomb
On Earth, you're beneath the sun and moon
Intuition stays in tune.

Mother Nature repels a destructive hand,
Or a species that destroys her humble land.
Life is cosmic, sensitive, it's not a misfit.
Our only tool kit.

Bird, turtle, flower, man,
Dolphin, bear, tiger, lamb.
All heartbeats equal, all in the dance,
Dawning days beam romance.
If humans really are the species stronger than all,
Why do we then watch each other fall
On fields and in homes, the catastrophe of war
There are free, life-saving resources to adore.
Enlightened with facts to later ignore.

Slow-kill, cancerous, foods
Fed to brain and body as if there's nothing to lose.
Taxes, anxiety, corruptors, news,

Engineered to distort, to confuse.
Consumerism, ego, perfume, cars,
Watered down music in ethanol bars.
Social class, wages, money, competition,
Illicit propaganda leaking from your television.
Left-wing, right-wing, blue, yellow, red.
Vote for us, depend on us – democracy is underfed.
Either that or its game's in one's head.
What other approaches can evolution take instead?

Resources supporting our basic needs.
Renewable energy: wind, tide, wave and sun,
More time for fun.
Sense of reason unified, positivity in abundance,
A clean conscience
Slavery system – a thing of the past.
Poverty, scarcity addressed at last.
Gut-feelings pursued, progress piece by piece
Lessons learnt; ignorance ceased.
Declines in anger and fear,
Acceptance brings people near.
Know the power of perception,
Question the illusion of perfection,
Productive reflection,
Then peace from the start,
Have faith the mind is in the heart.

IT'S YOU

It's your eyes that attract me
Your eyes that relax me
The way your face says yes
It's you, it's you.

It's your voice that speaks like a singing bird
The sound where my dreams are only heard
The whisper of an Angel says yes
It's you, it's you.

It's your soul that has really taken me
Never thought I'd meet anyone just like me
Happiness is easy when I'm with you
It's you, it's you.

-

Today I questioned the sea:
"Why do you constantly reach out to me?
Is it my dreams you seek or my homeland?
Let it be said,
You may take either within the warm crest of your wave.
Only on the condition
That I am then stolen, and too,
As blue and as beautiful as you."

HIM AND HER

Standing here,
I can see the love of him and her.
The children, the family, the friends.
The effort, the work, the spend.
Their past, their journey until now
And their future, the gift of their vow.

I don't know if it was love at first sight.
But I was lucky enough to witness their light
In the early stages.
As they kindled and kissed.
A sight not to be missed
As they both fell in love at their own speed
It was clear then that each other are all that they need.

For him, never to settle or commit
Until he was certain of the right fit.
To soften him
And build his empire bit by bit.
For her, choices were made
Her heart unafraid,
The butterfly sensation stayed
As she considered a bridesmaid.

Standing here,
I see how they've nurtured children.
The thought, the care,
The teamwork, the share.

They teach us that wealth isn't held by a billionaire.
It's held in our hearts and our gut.
I see the growth of a family tree.
A community, a brotherhood,
From childhood to adulthood
An English tradition understood.
Thank you to him
Thank you to her
For reminding us all, it's love we prefer.

ENGLAND! OH ENGLAND!

England oh England
Womb of my heart,
Native fighter
Never to part,
Show seasons,
Of all colour and dew,
Forever giving reasons
To live above you.

England oh England
Upon your soil I stand,
Passion, awe, legacy
Engraved in your hand,
Chronologies of memories
In your graceful land.

Tread softly little island,
Don't let time forget triumphs
Unity with Welsh and Scot!
Oh Albion!
Oh Caledonia!
Oh Cymry!
Our magic island and witty tongues
Are cuddled by water!
One body, not three!

ODE TO GRANDADS

Look, front window
Over crescent coastline
Daily nook, land meets water
Backdrop of stories, river of thoughts.

Croaky voice reciting traditions
How times have changed
Understanding New England.

The mill gone
Vows now different
The news entertains you
No longer informs you.

Ballroom dances still exist
So does true love.
A map your reading

Or the order of old kings.
Your diet cannot be that bad if you're 92.
The kids have it tough nowadays.
Look, it's the man with the guide dog.
They must be testing the church bells.
One World War and one World Cup
One job lasting 40 years
One family, one son, one wife, one life.

Look, front window
Over crescent coastline,
Final years,
Feel the old nostalgia
Of the early days
The Merseyside docks,
Big ships, Atlantic bound.
The tickle to go back may never leave
Like your instinct to believe
To have faith,
Good Christian that you are
Disciplined not discoloured
Devoted not weighed down
In your lounge
You are king and crown.
Bricks of your home, will forever recite:
"Where's me' bloody stick?
What is app?
People speak too fast nowadays
Give the cat a goldfish
Count your blessings."

Cast a ripple on a ray
Of law-abiding light.
Watch it cripple everyday
All obscenities in sight.

Watch the spell jeer and toy
All weakness in its way.
Then you´ll be wise, full of joy
As you see out your day.

WIDE SMILES OF LONDON

Whilst drinking upon London's forgotten streets,
Dripping tongues laugh and tell.
The secrets of enjoyment,
Revelations of a wishing well.

Many a working day has called for this,
Fulfilment of wild desire.
Many a tomorrow has wept for this,
Memories of joy, smiles and fire.

Capital pints serve capital charm,
Sipped, sung, cheers of bliss.
Not one bystander put at harm,
Not one second to miss.

Stories written here,
This realm of now.
Days to hold inside forever,
For as long as the heart can allow.

Busy streets, busier taps,
Pour sun into smiley men of play.
The great city spins on,
In its own creative way.

These alehouses have tret many a soul,
The Ripper, Todd, Raleigh and Wilde.
Footprints engraved upon the ground,
All grief meek and mild.

Soon the boys of wide smiles will leave,
Returning to nests by the sea.
Bearing scars of joy,
Remembering misery, the absentee.

THE WIND

Today, wind asked:
"Why separate and let magic die
From that girl with seashell eyes?
Skin of silk, so splendidly soft,
A mermaid from the North Sea of Lowestoft."

I answered:
"Separate, I did not!
Nor her, nor beast or temptress!
Twas you; wind, who blew hearts astray!
Both now lost!
Forced to alter, to bid farewell
To our home-grown wishing well!"

Wind loitered,
Turned, cried:
"True, I must confess
Destiny diversified.
Sometimes love and fortune
Has no shelter to hide.
Sometimes there is no harbour
From the tide of time,
And no shield
To parry fruits of fire."

WHEN TWO LOVERS MEET

Two stood as one on a sandy beach
Evening walking so fine, so sweet.
Held his breath; said three magic words
First time they've ever been heard.
Life is sweet when two lovers meet.

She strokes his skin with her tender left hand
Looks into his eyes, she's found her man.
Kissing and rolling through gold sand
As happy as can be.
The sea it speaks so gracefully
Hearts beating impatiently.
Colours shine above their heads
Kisses on repeat.
Life is sweet when two lovers meet.

Music flows from halos and eyes
Opportunities ahead, children could rise.
Light blinds as clouds drift apart
Hand in hand they walk;
The long way home, more time for them both
To exchange words for spirit and growth.
Not long until he's leaving her again
Duties overseas.
Life is sweet when two lovers meet.

Weeks pass, away from each other
Only memories where they see their lover.

Reminds himself that everything's fine
He's just got to wait his time.
She wonders if he's dreaming of her
Wants his warmth just like they once were.
Reminds herself, everything's fine
She's got to wait her time.
Life is sweet when two lovers meet.

UNITY

As I'm my foot, I'm the earth.
Wind rustles leaves, lungs exhale.
Eyelids drop, moon rises.
As rivers carry water,
Life circulates artery.

Petals blossom upon crown of head.
Hearts beat as waves shuttle
Eyelids rise, moon falls.
Trees grow from the root
Life branches out.

Money doesn't grow on trees.
It's not created by mother nature, it's not her expertise.
Was made by man, for his need.
Or to profit, or to strengthen greed.
Behold the flower in the garden,
As well as the weed.

WHEN WILL SHE COME HOME

Like a swallow bellowing from a tree
Her rhymes of love call out to me.
But now she's invisible, no longer there to see,
She fled during a storm, away flew my destiny.

Blow your kiss as I blow mine
There is love but no time.
Don´t break my heart, don't guillotine the divine,
Suffering in the sorrow of separation.

When will she come home?
I've been sitting here waiting all alone
When will she come home?

Waiting for her knock-knock on my door
I´ve been here too many times before,
When will she come home?

THE WAITING

The waiting.
I've been waiting too long.
Hating every song
That I've been playing.
It's amazing

What two eyes can do to you
To make a broken heart
Play healing through the day.
What can I say?
Tomorrow seems too far away.
Need to pass the time today.
Need a reason why I'm living this way.
Need explanations of the constant complications
And the thoughts I struggle to convey.
I've been praying and contemplating
Whilst the lovers in heart have been mating,
Romantically debating
It's best to hold onto,
The waiting.

The waiting.
Knocks on your door
At quarter to four in the morning
Does it make you boring?
If you enjoy a little time on your own.
Curl up by the fireplace in your home
Hold the one you love who's tired of being alone.
Take her heart from the start
Remind her she's the one that you now own.
My, how you have grown
Honesty is the only arrow I have thrown.
But, when the wind changes direction
I'll be right back here contradicting my intention.
Was that your expectation of me?
How much longer will it take for you to see

That patience is the key
The gift to enable us to be free.
That's why I've been praying and contemplating
Whilst the two lovers in my hearts have been mating.
And romantically debating
That it's best to hold onto,
The waiting.

-

Wisdom sleeps
Within the space between each word
Music in the gaps
That silent tone
Waiting to be filled.

LITTLE BIT OF LOVE

A little bit of love, early morning
Little bit more, sun starts yawning
Then twice as much as I rest my sleepy head.
Little bit of love gives a little bit of love.

Pretty little flower dancing in the garden
Sways with the wind never begs his pardon,
For stealing attention with his colourful petals and pearls.
A little bit of love gives a little bit of love.

A little bit of love as we stare at stars
Play favourite songs on air guitars,
Tiny things, bring a little smile to me.
Little bit of love gives a little bit of love.

Mister Starling cruising through the sky
Got his own free will, needs no alibi,
Wish I had wings, to fly like him.
Little bit of love gives a little bit of love.

RECOLLECTIONS

I once slept
With a bride by my side
Her smile constant and fair.
Though a bitter disease
Made her fall to her knees
Now my bed is empty and bare.

I think, I cry
For reasons why,
Why she was stolen from hand.
No sense made of this
Only pain and risk
Existence hard to withstand

But no!
Not me, a loser in fight!
A complaint or fake disguise!
I´ll take all I've learnt,
Beaten and burnt
Fuel for final reprise.

TO FUN

Out forth you must go
Into that gentle wind
Remember the funny faces though
Those who giggled and grinned!

Up! Onwards! Into the fun!
Swirl in natures law
Bonding mind to eye
Numb the need for more!

Tickle a smile, pinch a nerve
Tease a tongue or two
Poke fun, show the sun
Abundances to do!

Whittle worries, ease the heart
See the pleasures of play
Clean the slate, do debate
Joys yet found today!

A dawn sleeps near, gems shine
Beneath this clouded veil
Let secrets be, may lovers see
Their fire, flag and grail,

UNREST

Don't know what I feel about you
Don't know if it's love or hate around you
Unrest, my heart's in unrest.

Don't know why it's like this
Don't know why I despise this
Unrest, my heart's in unrest.

I need help right now
Guide me somehow
Unrest, my heart's in unrest.

I still see your eyes that make my heart dance
I still see your eyes that make dark clouds shine
I wish things were easy
I hope they will be one day
The day when love washes the pain away
Unrest, my heart's in unrest.

This pen shows my thoughts,
Reads my mind then makes notes.
Speaks the words my mouth can't say,
I cherish this pen in every way.

MY LITTLE SECRET

If nature has her way, I´ll be left alone today
Distant on a cloud that rains sorrow.
If temptation has his say, I´ve lost resilience anyway
Faith in the invisible I will follow,
But will I be too late tomorrow?

Do you hear vocation call?
When you sleep does your spirit fall?
Into hands that surround your worried mind.
Hope stands tall, but truth is small
Long way to go before you know it all,
But half-way there you might find what you came looking for.

Confusion begs a hand,
Sense reminds where we stand
Night lights shine bright in the morning.
Life may soon change its plan,
Remember the road from which you ran,
No reason to beg, steal or borrow.
But will I be too late tomorrow?

I don't dare say, lover never let me go.
Because you're my little secret – locked inside my heart
My little secret – holding my hand through it all
My little secret – sharing impossible dreams
My little secret – time to wake up, so it seems.

-

Patience we´ll hold
As chores will take,
Our days from pleasure and play.
But lose we won´t
Or fail to make
Smiles to keep frowns at bay.

SPLENDID THINGS

Hands be gentle as heart is strong
Grant peace in this ever long
Shining ray of light that's blinding.

Dedicated souls will make it through
Harder life gets the more we do
Love as a religion on the lifelong avenue.

If all is empty, make it full
Light a day that's dull.
Forgive, forget, mistakes we made
Ascend, past can fade.

Between your heartbeat and mine
A chime bell rings,
It rings, for splendid things.

FOUR SEASONS

Autumn's gust
Spawning leaves
Scatter, see
Untouched territory.

Winter's blizzard
Crystal ice
White at night
Hygge delight.

Spring's songs
Hymn birds
Rainbow drops
Sunshine knocks.

Summer's smile
Creatures small
Golden shine
Extended time.

WALK WITH ME

Spending time thinking about you
Let love free my mind.
Our faces in places we've never been
But in my dreams, there's no landmark we haven't seen.

Are you brave enough for the truth?
If feelings return, are we foolish or will we learn
Maybe we're meant to be,
Lessons grant chance to irradicate catastrophe.

So close yet so far away,
If I could hold your soul,
There's only one thing I would say
Walk with me
Brighter shades of life, our loving side will see.
Walk with me
Make tonight go on for eternity.
Walk with me
And I'll take my chance to show how much you mean to me,
Walk with me.

SIDE BY SIDE

We´ve been saying these words,
Thinking these thoughts,
A thousand million times.
A heart beats inside you,
When you do
The magic that circles your mind.

We´ve been walking this road
Letting our love unfold
As both our souls repent.
Form a plan with your pen,
You'll know where you stand
As the future's etched into your skin.
Love through the tough times
Love through the good times
Love through the times we´re not even there.
Love me in worry
If we´ve got no money
You know I'll be there for you.

You're one of a kind
So glad I met someone like me.
Wherever you go, whatever you see
I´ll be in your shadow subconsciously.
Whatever you learn, whatever you do
I´ll be side by side with you.

-

I remember her cosmic eyes
And voice of sea and wind.
Unsure of her origin
Or what European town she twinned.

But I do recall her touch
And kiss of wicked flair.
Yet still I question her morality
And if she was ever there.

-

When you smile, smile some more
Like you did, many times before.
Don't give in, don't give up
Don't turn around or tear life up
It's in our hands, we make our luck,
Make it good and make it last.
So, when you smile; smile some more
Just like you did so many times before
Smile some more.

I WAS A CAT

I was a cat in a previous life
Nine lives they were my saviour.
Not a worry in this hurried world
My days they posed no danger.

Mice, dogs, fleas, open doors
Eating time then sleeping time.
Cat flap fun then clawing floors
Stealthily viewing all kinds of crime.

-

When you are old
And you are nodding off by the fireplace
With distant memories on your face,
I'll be holding your hand.

FREE BIRDS

Two white doves flew over me, singing in harmony
Alongside robins and rustling of the trees.
Destiny forged a path to walk
With you in my heart and mind.
I prayed and hoped
One day not too far from now
We both would share these sounds.

You and I were born free birds
Let our wings kiss the clouds.

I marched through fields and lakes, searching for you,
Climbed a mountain for eight days, sixteen storms I soldiered through.
Listening to a drive and a gut feeling inside.
If I lost faith in this, I would have fallen, I could have died
Instead I arrived, I sang and shouted loud.
I hoped you were nearby,
So, you could hear the echoed sounds.
You and I were born free birds
Let our wings kiss the clouds.

She heard my call then in she flew, wings flapping from the west.
I felt her warmth, her touch, then her kiss.
Then we flew away together
Making up for time we had missed.
My journey, my test, alas reached a sacred end.
Now we plan the life we intend to spend.
Two making one, creating a little crowd,
You and I were born free birds
Let our wings kiss the clouds.

\-

For a world that's gone
A new world is born.
And built upon the same soil and ashes
As the foundations of time.
The roads lead back
To where we come from,
For better, for worse.

\-

If heart loves
Without rules or remorse
Don't fear the knives of light,
Or wild words.
To run is to die.
So, if heart raves
Without condition or expectation
Do not block the diamond air
To turn is to lie
To heart and mind.
Hands bored, unscathed
Days trapped as sleep.

-

Sometimes sun, sometimes rain
Sometimes the thing you never expected again.
Sometimes happiness, sometimes pain
Sometimes loss in order to gain.

-

Celebrate everything.
Day
Breath
Dawn
Death.

STAFFIES IN THE SCHOOLYARD

Staffies in the schoolyard
At home, foul language on a plate.
Mockery by abusive parents,
Passion for hate to marinate.
Kids locked into an education system that starts too late.
Fuelled by seats and sugar drinks
Ensuring classmates can't concentrate.

Staffies in the schoolyard
Smartphones instead of brains.
Pornographic music, Facebook constraints.
Reducing the will to fulfil romance on first dates.
Why do many feel out of place?
Analyse not, prepare for rat race.

Staffies in the schoolyard
Cheap cider in dad's carrier bag.
He staggers at the school gates,
Shirt dirty, negativity to brag.
Cursing children as he flicks his fag,
Whinge, whinge, whinge, nag, nag, nag.

Staffies in the schoolyard,
Division in the air.
Assumptions constant, death stare, evil glare,
Directed to a minority's face, race or hair.
Curse, snigger, insult, stare,

It seems many skived the classes on equality and care.

Staffies in the schoolyard,
Ungoverned home-learning too.
Parents play vulgar teachers,
Bruises turn blue.
Vocation-killers, screen addiction, apathy, hate,
Confusion, fear, reliance on the state.

Staffies watch these children grow,
In this torturous environment of struggle and woe.
Quietly observing day by day,
A decline in smiles, a decline in play.
Where is the happiness that was here yesterday?
Where are the dreams of the young?
Where is purity to end this disarray?
How long will their songs be unsung?

THE BALLAD OF JEFFERSON AND MCLEAN

Jefferson and Mclean shared the same dream.
Conditioned minds sold into the world of war,
Misled by propaganda, career ladder hard to ignore.
Little did they know,
Puppet masters of the world,
Regimes of corruption
Adverts promoting one view.
They didn´t think twice
Believed lies were true.

What did the adverts say?
"Fight for your country!
Blood! Honour! Pride!
We´ll give you brotherhood
And a conscience to hide!
Come forth, risk life!
Forget harm.
Fulfil policy
Raise panic alarms.
Prepare to be killed
For no-one but us.
Brave and bold
Do what you're told.
You're a serviceman
Not a toy of the trade.
Don't think you're a murderer
Because out here it's okay."

Jefferson and Mclean; war made them mates,
Convinced that heroism is a safe, happy place.
Shipped out across shore
To a land they didn't know.
Battlefield for a home.
Cold pit for a bed.
Few loud words were said
Followed by a slap around the head.
Time to kill somebody or die trying.

They loaded guns
Crouched, took aim.
Froze for a moment,
They remembered again.
That they were once young
Free with desire.
No fear of anything
Anywhere, anyone.
It was then they remembered
That their value was higher.
Mystified as to where this idea had begun.

"What are we doing?"
One said to the other.
"What am I meant to do?
Kill someone then make it two?
I was once a man of morals and love.
My actions have sworn!
General, take back your guns
And so-called uniform!

Tears fill my eyes
From the hell I have seen!
How do I become clean
From this obscene machine?
Why are we even here?
Only a minority know.
We´re puppets following orders,
Fuelling the evening news show!
How do those warmongers look so clean?
Hiding behind ties.
There's blood on their hands
But still they plot further plans."

Jefferson and Mclean
Dropped their guns and turned away.
But upon fleeing,
Poor Mclean was struck.
A bullet through his head.
A shot of bad luck.
Jefferson carried him away,
Thinking of McLean's family
And the words he would say.

"I regret to inform
Your son has been killed.
In a field of war
I'm yet to learn what for.
But I wouldn't blame the villain
Who inflicted the gunshot.
Look to global leaders

Who ensure that war doesn't stop.
The fake democracy warriors
Who instigate with mouth and pen.
Send them out on the battlefield
And let their families feel
What it's like,
To never see their loved ones again."

TRIBUTE TO GRAFTERS

Sunrise - grafters rise, meet
Labour, cause, their mercy seat.
Sweat, force and toil
Down the mine - turmoil.

The lost shaft underground
Obscurity, only sound,
Axe hammerings, grunts, woe.
Oh, how dim life can glow.

End, rise to light
Wash eyes, reclaim sight.
Behold earth, bright in way
Trot home, sleep, another day.

Tommy Smith: innocent at nine,
Worries Mum by weeping all the time.
Cough, dark as death itself,
Raises a concern in juvenile health.

Cleaned, fed, tucked in bed that night,
Mum trusted he´d heal alright.
But during Tom's sleep, mineshaft came,
To keep him in darkness for labour again.

YOU BE THE BOOK

You be the book
Every word, every sentence
Every page
Read you will
Rush
Glance
Snails meander the inner voice
Steady hand
Turn
Scan
Gist, detail
Sway attention
Read aloud
You be the book
Every word, every sentence
Every page
Every second, every hour
Every day
You are the story
You be the book.

CIVILLIAN CASUALTY

Confusion when viewing the evening news!
Common sense bemused!
President of State sadistically irate,
Threatening with outlandish views.

It's nothing new to see on the flat-screen TV,
Because war is apparently the way for us to be.
But things hit me to provoke my thought,
This behaviour wasn't stated when people put forward their vote.
War, a deception that many seem to understand,
But what the news said
Stirred a tormented truth in my head.

The presenter said, a bombing display
Stole livelihoods away,
Home and shelter as well.
Civilians dead whilst sleeping in bed,
Justified by military personnel.

But this was not a war, not a battle
Of two sides in air, land and sea.
Instead an act of sin
From an order of the highest decree.

Still the world waits for the criminals' trial to begin.
But there's not a second thought,
No room for questions within

An ungovernable order and rule.
Therefore, where is justice?
Which breach of law should I quote?
I've given up on answers.
How do I withdraw my vote?

DIGITAL HANDCUFFS

Listen young one,
Smartphone has got your wrists and digits.
Blue light has caught your eye.
'Likes' have got you wanting
Even though they make you shy.

Your hand picks it up automatically,
Eyesight is blinkered too.
Can you remember an emotional response?
Or a vocation to live and do?

You've missed out on the greenery
No earth and soil in your nails.
All of Mother Nature's scenery
All the unexplored trails.

Place the digital handcuffs in the fire,
Or at least in the drawer.
Then feel the energies around you,
There are miracles and more!

BLACK AND WHITE

Black and white is what we're conditioned to hear,
Poisoning minds, inflicting fear,
Inner turmoil causing tears,
Humanity has seen throughout the years.

Black and white is in the street,
In trees where birds meet.
Black and white is born in every country every day,
Resist or accept, it's here to stay.

Black versus white on the evening news,
Preference, obedience, divisive views,
Taxpayers money to help abuse,
Perception of colour, a face to accuse.

What choices did you make about the colour of your skin?
You spawned from a vagina into a loony bin.
What matters is the person within,
But if it's torment behind their grin,
It's them that will suffer for their sin,
Then it's the story of black and white all over again.

Some cry, some laugh,
As nutcases divide the world we have.
For the masses it's wrong but for some it's right,
Why do we fight between black and white?

POLITICIANS PARTY

There's a politician's party going on in the town,
No chairs for people to sit down.
Hid away deep underground,
So far away we never hear a sound.

I saw a street dweller outside there earlier
Lost in life, occupation beggar.
Pleading for small change,
Homeless, hungry, wounded by weather.

"Please," he asked a nearby suit,
"Pennies for food."
The suit sniggered with disgust at his will to intrude
As he walked away, he giggled and snarled.
Leaving need on the ground with neither penny nor pound
There's a politician's party going on in the town.

What is discussed at this democratic disco?
Honesty of vows or changes achieved?
Prestige blazers or silk ties?
Admittance of failures or confessions to lies?

Will they discuss the beggar sat outside?
Criticise poverty or his spirit lost inside?
Debate legacy handed down to the youth

Or the shape of young minds?
Do they attempt to unify the world we find?
There's a politician's party going on the town.

Now many question how much good of what we see is new.
Agendas influence newspapers, TV and radio too.
Is it really all about strife, loss or liberties withdrew
Love is more important to Earth than war that's true.

We hope politicians find peace,
United, a shared faith that it is safer to cease,
From thoughts of control and the need to kill.
Instead, comforting humans and honesty with the unpayable debt bill.

There's a politician's party going on in the town,
No chairs for people to sit down.
Hid away deep underground,
So far away we never hear a sound.

ODE TO GUY FAWKES

Resistance, revolution and shock
Forced Big Ben to fall.
Eels of the Thames now surround London's clock
Inciting nerves in the palace of Whitehall.

Ben was attacked by plot and snare
Exploded by divided hearts within.
Punished by rebels opting not to play fair
Their patience grown desperately thin.

Ministers raged, newspapers spoke
Of terrorists who scarred honest land.
Scorn poured on a wild Catholic bloke
His prophecies illegal and banned.

As Big Ben slept with the English fish
Few cad London minds breathed power and hope.
So, lawmen cut every thoughtful wish
As rogues were dropped via noose and rope.

WORLD GONE CRAZY

World gone crazy,
Time gone mad,
Hand signed paper,
War victim sad.

Shell killed child,
Morality lost,
Norm feels odd,
Line been crossed.

Truth deleted,
Mind control intact,
Money is nature,
Lie is fact.

Lost common ground,
Deception is polite
Lunatics in power,
Purpose lost sight.

Price too high,
Baby underfed,
Job shut down,
Machine instead.

Dumb down youth
Opposition there,
TV magnet,
Watch, listen, stare.

Fear near doorstep,
Danger beyond wall,
Resources very short,
Planet too small.

World gone crazy,
Time gone mad,
Man made monster,
God gone sad.

FIGHT AMONGST THEMSELVES

There's not a lot of love in the city lights
Instead, drugs, chlamydia and drunken fights
But it doesn't matter if addiction's right
Because we´ve all still got to go out tonight
To wear what we're sold
But not what we are
Because after a few, we´re all rock hard
Drive borrowed Jaguars
Big ego stars
Paralytic in clubs and bars
Play air guitars
Give police the 'large´
All the local celebrity stars are out tonight
Tell yourself it's alright
You keep it going,
But one day it will start showing
Then even you will believe in knowing
There's not a lot of love in the city lights
Instead drugs, chlamydia and drunken fights.

Look outside the night club window
Do you see what I see too?
Can you see the pain-ridden anger?
And propaganda they live through?
Do you see the destroyed dreams?
And delusions that were never true?
Let them fight amongst themselves
Because I'm weary - just like you.

SUFFOLK'S SEAGULL FORTRESS

Suffolk's seagull fortress
On look out with imperial eyes.
Defending Britannia´s borders and her treaty
From intruder or revolutionary rise.

Father Gull gazes into easterly winds
Overlooking shore and nation.
Beside his queen and children,
His feathered air force who await consultation.

Stillness, the waiting, years pass and then:

English tranquility falls
A panic siren calls.
Gulls screech to each other with heed
Winged armies alight to fulfil their need.

It's a sound that the homeland fear to hear
Look! The horizon! A hostile armada is drawing near!
By the hour, North Sea reels the imposters in
An altercation, soon to begin.

So, the aviation warning parade soar south
Singing their way to Westminster.
To alert the prime minister of the unwelcome visitor
And a sinister brigade that they bring.

A miraculous sight within the grounds of parliament.
Over two thousand birds sing strong.

Stillness, the waiting, hours pass and then:

Alas! The powers that be, have heard!
And with a noble word
An investigation into the bellowing birds.

A militant check of sea and air,
Then a discovery off the coast of East Anglia
Most unusual and rare.

Ghostly war ships!
Oncoming threats in sight!
Homeland mortars deployed to fight!
Righteous carnage throughout the night!

Albion's birds return to the east
Their duty done,
Together they look on.

Suffolk's seagull fortress
On look out with imperial eyes.
Defending Britannia's borders and her treaty
From intruder or revolutionary rise.

LEILA

Leila, oh, Leila
In East Anglia will see her
Riding through rivers and rough northern seas.
Leila oh Leila,
Aged, vintage and freer
Than any soul or vessel in God's fine blue land.

She's a raw, damp old girl,
As wet as she's rough.
Liberating camaraderie,
No crew that isn't tough.

She spits in the eye
Of high-class company.
Independently ruthless,
Ropes, knots and trees.

Leila oh Leila
East Anglia will see her,
Riding through rivers and rough northern seas.
Leila oh Leila,
Aged, vintage and freer
Than any soul or vessel in Gods fine blue land.

IF THE PRESIDENT

If the President were to sleep the streets alone
Would chief of state see?
Amidst rats, stench and dirt
The truth about equality.

Because from this viewpoint,
Some classes seem intolerantly unfair,
Eager to point the finger,
Rarely the heart to care.

If out of sight is out of mind
Why should one partake,
In conversations of woe
When policy is at stake.

Should we enslave, steal, take,
Or buy all of which one can?
Fast competition in the western world
Hinders the collective concern of man.

What is a lesson of equality?
Is it to lay the president in the hunger huts
Where offspring lay dead and bare?
No flesh on the bone
No water or food to share.

Or is it for the minister to scream
Beneath the aftermath of an attack drone,
Without limbs, walls or guards,
Human rights left unknown.

If the president were to sleep the streets alone
Would chief of state be able to see?
Amidst rats, stench and dirt
The truth about equality.

BENEATH THE SPRINKLES OF MIRACLE HYMN

Beneath the sprinkles of miracle hymn,
A world of what was has changed.
Undoing evil knots
Creates seeds of hope,
And graves for ugly spells.

Angelic tear ducts throw rain,
Cleansing ears, eyes and mouth.
Pardoning warlords
For massacres of heart and world,
Divinity in the breath.

Stars fall from greedy races,
Verse and rhyme synchronise clouds.
Evolving jail houses to faith houses,
Whore houses to family houses
And corrupt houses to dust.

Lightening dazzles from the golden words
Whispered by God himself.
Crystal for brick, silence for noise.
Centuries on, change does not grow thin,
Beneath the sprinkles of miracle hymn.

MAN MUST NOT RUSH HIS CRAFT

Man must not rush his craft
Or folly the heart's harvest.
Let be, loves seasonal course
Of gel, bond and juice.
Within the tranquil nest of life
May the breath be patient.
Man must not rush his craft.

Man must not rush his craft
Nor forge an act that is not his.
A vessel for the letting of life
Resistance obsolete.
Vocal heartbeats
Trot gently aside cryptic speed.
Man must not rush his craft.

Man must not rush his craft
Trophies of death will be spoilt.
Legacies lost; words misplaced

A whirling ghost in the air.
May care aide every move
Weave the cotton of the soul.
Man must not rush his craft.

WHEN A HERO

When a hero comes as a hero surely must
And her healing skin tickles your loving wounds
Drink from her cup of completion
Take happy refuge in her lifelong safehouse
Take your heart and its mind to her innermost isle
Towards the unsung abyss of her love
Within the clean trenches of her romance
And into the infinite ocean of her eyes
Here, share your rations,
Make your own little platoon
Watch the troops rally to the sound of her gentle song
Then, on a grey, empty Thursday afternoon
Feel yourself deeper in her arms than ever before
As she cradles your past, present and future
With her palms.

When a hero warms as a hero surely must
Let her fire help you to your feet
Believe in the confidence of her ideas
As they shape your road
And photosynthesize family tree.
Take your labour and time to her innermost isle

Embrace a wisdom you long to learn
And a view you hope to breathe
So, by taking her hand in marriage
Two heroes become one
Victories shared
Triumphs swapped
Children lionized
And a home forever gifting peace.

-

To you dear colleague, I have lost a job.
To you prevailing landlord, I have lost a home.
To you deceitful neighbour, I have lost a wife.
Yet, I thank you all for this poem.

WHITE INK

White ink stains the pages of declarations
Without notification or limitation
White ink plagues the page
Veiled in hope
White ink steals life and rights.
Says what isn't said
Beside the black ink
White ink carries time
Holds it just the same
Lessons clenched, as if to pass on
Science passed

Art handed
In many a doctrine and law
Invisible ink is used.

A GAME OF CARDS

A game of cards is being played,
Where dramatic stakes are being laid.
Drones, propaganda, threats to invade,
For whom has the most power, there's profit to be made.

Every nation plays a hand,
The house deals and commands
But if you can't raise or meet the demand,
Fold your cards and give up your hand.

They play the game around large tables,
Handshakes with foes; some old, some new.
Bluffing with distractions, distorting world view,
Poker faces high, blind and wild.

As we observe this game of cards
The eye of truth see's right through.
Some have a conscience in need of review
Because the hand they hold is far from true.

JAIL CELL

Jail cell, jail cell,
Living hell,
Alive or dead you just can't tell,
Claustrophobic morbid shell,
Lost count how many times I rang the bell.

Jail cell, jail cell
The hole where bravery fell,
Conscience and karma feels unwell,
Sin has a funny smell,
No such thing as a wishing well.

Jail cell, jail cell,
Nobody hears you yell,
Dull, freebie hotel,
Makes your head swell
Reality bombshell
Another tale to tell.

Jail cell, jail cell,
Few things parallel,
Everything to dwell,
Emotional carousel,
At the mercy of the policy cartel,
They treat you very well,
Animal food and a book by George Orwell.

Jail cell, Jail cell,
Enjoys a farewell,
It's a bloody hard sell,
No use to a gazelle,
Lairy clientele,
To some, the infidel,
Attract then repel,
Heed this intel.

WE REGRET TO INFORM

We regret to inform,
The execution of your family tree,
Smoke replaces the name
Of the boy who was once to carry your arms,
As well as your gene pool.

Songs of honour fled his lungs,
Upon kissing the wet red soil.
Verity clenched in prayer,
A sacrifice of what was.
Ghost of service lives on,
His shadow now underground.

Proud, not mournful, you are expected to be,
In response to this thundering news.
You are blessed by immortal glory,
That death was forced early
In making our cause valiant.

The reason of his feud is known to all,
For safety within your sleep.
To engulf my valleyed desires,
Pretending to erase enemies,
Enforcing future penny and lingo.

But don't despair, all is not lost for you,
Behold the bloodied medal inside.
Neighbours will marvel,
Causing smiles within tears,
And envy to boys of nothing.
 -

Back then, we sang songs of freedom
Grinned whilst grafting for a future.
Chiselling the foundations
For those who later denied us bread, water and love.
We knuckled so hard that our eyes became void
Blank of pupil, null in life.

Then came the dawning of a new era.
The pride and cause of our labour
Visions of fields and light.
Now look at us
Look into our eyes
Look deeper
Look.
Do you see the sun?
Do you?

THE MASTER OF DISGUISE

Menacing mortars molested my home
Prayer sang from hands.
Streets oozed fury
Serenaded by marching gun bands.
No escape or reassurance of will
No rain to cloud his rise.
We voted for him then cheered for him:
The Master of Disguise.

Brainwash me, hypnotise me
Crush all that is strong.
Confuse me, then enslave me
For recovering from wrong.
In youth I was taught
To abandon sin and lies.
That's all I ever see of you
The Master of Disguise.

Law isn't law, if creators are breakers
And takers of finance and land.
Does truth offend
The act of your hidden hand?
Halos are cultivating
How now to galvanize?
Control is slowly crumbling for
The Master of Disguise.

A MAN ONCE SOUGHT TO OWN

A man once sought to own
Globes and hearts that were not his.
Theft of history upon native land
Agony within homeland bricks.
Behold the intrusive renovation tanks,
And thrones draped in warm, red vile.

A speech once sought to chain
Desire of divine
To dispel fruits
To tell the wind, love is not one.
Emptiness watches these spells of null
As dream-eaters feast upon the soul.

Flags turn to flames
People scalded by pen.
Tongues scrunched and censored,
No tears left to shed.
Brush away the unwanted bone
A man once sought to own.

DARK CLOUDS

Bury me, dark clouds
Take time with your smoke-filled mirrors
Upon cascading tyrant height.
Force one beneath dark cloth
Into arcadia disguised as night.

Enlighten me, dark clouds
Why so passive, vast and free?
What is now, was not then?
Why offer vision,
If unable to see?

Answer me, dark clouds
What sense do you bring?
Upon an England misled in vain.
An opening makes sense for your two-sided conscience
To present us with light once again.

HOLLOW COUNTRYLAND

Hollow countryland
Be you a love
Or be you a burden
Why such horror in your grin
Why dark demise under arrogant eyes
Of an empire falling within

Be you youth
Or be you age
Be you the daily reporting of rage
Be you the same voice and book
That educates us up
For chaos to later upstage.

Hollow countryland
Be you a start
Or be you an end
Be you the time that I spend
Of a ghostly life prolonged
Are you the right that I have wronged.

CULTURE SHIFT

Sanity is success
Progress a pratfall
Reproduction a risk,
Future a fix.

Service is slavery
Education an error
Community a concern,
Status a sin.

Aging an anxiety
Entertainment an eyesore
News, a nightmare,
Screens a substance.

Divides are dominant
Companionship conditional
Love is foggy,
Greed is good.

Opinions operate
Compassion a curse
Duty, a deception,
Culture, a singularity.

ODE TO KING ALFRED FROM LUDLOW CASTLE

Tis that ancient cymree
Beyond those gulping hills
For King Alfred awaits,
King of the West Saxons!
See him rally and bellow!
Fear much those of Jute and Dane
Your numbers may be many
Yet your land is far!

FIREHAND

Scalded truths are born
Propelled by the blazing opinion of firehand.
Devil-haired fingers carve the way
To extinct men of life and homeland.

Blankets of blood stain the ground
From a massacre launched by pen.
Driven by minds, lost within flags
Claiming defence once again.

Families torn, rogue ether,
Infinite problems in range
A power and class revel for now,
Ensuring things don't change.

THE SUN DID NOT SHINE IN

The orange circle burnt bright
But souls did not feel the light,
The sun did not shine in.
Failed illumination of the empty cells
Did not open stolen eyes.
Corpses aide symbols
As people patter themselves to dust.

Many acres held the pulseless numbers
Barbed barriers locked out the world,
The sun did not shine in.
In contrast, wolf-eyed boot men
Gulped the rays like wine.
As medals boast fear at play
Whilst overlooking the bare bodied rags.

Even though persecuted bones
Were alighted in smoke from the baron waste,
The sun did not shine in.
Darkness availed their memories

And told stories to grandchildren unborn.
Now free in the ether,
Roaming without concern.

Years pass and despite
Justice and redemption having their say,
The sun did not shine in.
When the evil minds ceased
And ascension was their play,
The architect had his say.
The sun did not shine in.

CITY MAN

Piercing gaze, radiant stride
Immaculate appearance
Well-spoken verbs
A grin that suits the city streets so well.
A voyager of tower blocks
The envy-eyed shoe shiner
Rubbing beneath a devil
Draped in the latest season of Prada.
Though we see flesh like ours,
Behind his unpausing mask
He briskly pasts us unaware.
We smell his aftershave
But behind his own closed doors
He is simply not there.

WEALTH

Some people perceive the local MP,
To be more vital than natures purity.
Referred to, more than creative energy,
More attention than vocational legacy.

Taxes, news, ownership, war.
Status, celebrity, must speak more.
Profits, corporations, business, votes,
Austerity, corruption, plastic bank notes.

Since when did headaches replace the power of space?
The songs of birds and nature's grace.
Colour, life, peace and health.
Where is a poor man found amongst such wealth?

JOURNEYING

Cruel can be the task of day
In slaving for forms of gold,
When the heart is worn and worked away
For doing what it's told.

Brass to earn his brass to eat
And a roof to shelter rain,
But a false life is your defeat
Your loss will be their gain.

There was once a time when coin and note
Nurtured art and stage,
When man and woman freely wrote
The beauties of their age.

And in that London lane
Where jesters once danced and played,
Slaves now hurry and pay in vain
With their souls for the taxation game.

So, when in that final bed you lay
And memories are all you hold,
Did you scar the earth with legacy?
Or live a life uncontrolled?

OLD GOEBBELS

Old Goebbels was a silly old soul
A silly old soul was he.
Controlling minds, controlling past
Redefining 'free'.

He thought a world would buy his word
To invest in his brothers of greed.
Until all did see a continent of blood
And that war was not of need.

His death, trivial, like his leaflets and films
Entrance and exit unique.
His propaganda fallen from shelf
Truth black and bleak.

But recycled, his remains were
Resurrected conventions now in control.
To influence minds and commit disguised crimes,
Fulfilling a new world order role.

UNWELCOME HYPROCRISY

9/11 was one of many terrible days
Of which day to day people were made to pay.
Hell flew in, uninvited from the skies
Hit down hard, drew blood to eyes.
It started as a vacation, all passports, all smiles
But landed the hard way as the world screamed for a while.
This is not meant to happen
This is not meant to be,
We are living as victims in an unwelcome hypocrisy.

Why fear and terror?
Why not unify together?
Why not address poverty,
And adapt to nature and weather?
But we don´t.
Same say it will stop but history says it won't,
Deception is widespread

Human minds are afloat.
Brainwashing is closer thaN you know
See for yourself on the evening news show.
This is not meant to happen
This is not meant to be,
We are living as victims in an unwelcome hypocrisy.

Narratives and agendas speak loud,
Evil acts proud
As the game goes on.
Negative messages, morphing beliefs
National representatives claim they want peace,
But arms trade doesn't cease.
Kill or be killed is an insane attitude
No love or respect in that,
No sense of gratitude.
How deadly is the bullet if all guns are destroyed?
War is tired – try something new.
Can peace be given a chance?
And if it doesn't work
Roll back to the bad old days,
But at least a species could have tried.
A clean conscience at least,
And saved some souls that would have died.
This is not meant to happen
This is not meant to be,
We are living as victims in an unwelcome hypocrisy.

THE DEVILS ANGEL

A windy evening in an old saloon
A game of cards under the shining moon.
High value on the table;
The gun of the Devil's Angel.

The barrel long, handle brown
The trigger gold, it ruled the town.
I won the game and got the gun
Power mine, on the run.

Some say it's a curse that fell from hell
An unforgiven sin you can never sell.
Whoever it's pointed at they've always fell
Fell to the hands of the Devil's Angel.

Time rolled by and I was fifty-nine
The Devils Angels still firing fine.
But that all changed when a visitor came
My spine tingled when it said its name.

I didn't get far until it pulled me back
Big red horns and the tail to match.
"*Give me my gun*", that's what it said
So, I aimed it straight and shot it dead.

BEHIND THE BLACK THAI SHACKS

Behind the black Thai shacks
What may breathe or lay?
For I see nothing but shadows
And life hidden from day.

Are there permanent sleepers' snakes or secrets?
Virus treasure or sin?
A portal hidden and tucked away
Or time capsules locked within?

There is a tattered shop
Which guards the frontal way
Owners who quarrel and talk
To act that all is OK.

Curious it makes my mind
To risk limbs and explore
My imagination cannot settle
My eyes demand for more.

So, pardon my absence
If for a lifetime I never come back,
I'll be investigating a world of nowhere
Behind the black Thai shacks.

WOMAN IN RED

Woman in Red
Drinks at the bar,
3 times a week
With men from afar.

Stunning presence
Striking sailors' eyes,
Some buy her drinks
Not to her surprise.

As sky turns black
The bar begins to clear,
The woman proposes an offer
He accepts with a cheer.

Her seductive ways
Has the prey chained up,
Helpless at her mercy
With the scent of blood.

Plunge with the carving knife
Slash of a butcher's,
For this murdering monster
Kills the men she touches.

Another night of torture and pain
The woman in red struck again,
Soon to be happily smoking tar

Not long until she returns to the bar.

-

The fear is only what stops you
What makes you wrong when right.
The fear will forever haunt you
And invade dreams at night.

Then in the morning when you yawn and wake
Fear takes you from the plans you were born to make.
Fear is the poison in a beautiful lake
Tread carefully of which road to take.

BURNLEY FC

Hear the earth-shaking roars of Burnley's mills and moors
Accompany the fans in the rain.
Bonded forever, yet together again
As a claret army in the beautiful game.

Chimneys watch on, many memories they hold
Alike with ancestors and dreams.
Alongside local grafters in Lancashire homes
Ready to duel rival teams.

Set upon by many an Englishman
Here to expect an easy ride.
Underestimating the underdog blood
Frequently leaving dissatisfied.

We are Burnley, super Burnley
A claret storm of passion and pride.
We are Burnley, super Burnley
Foot soldiers of the heroic Longside.

-

Language be the sword.
Meaning be the blade.
Form be the handle.
Melody be the grip.
Involution out.

STRIVE

Today I sighed at the sight of two men
Twinned in suit and shirt.
Discussing their strivings and goals
Both owning spines lined with knives.
Their evening meal
Like their hair strands - was perfect.
Their tone, convincingly assertive
As if straight from the life coaching manual.
Time ticked, they threw words

Shmuck glances mirrored the sun.
And as they threw their credit cards
I caught a brief glimpse of them harrowingly weeping.
A dark, grim halo cast no shadow
A void of which their plans and labour could never fill.
And as their working day ended
The day suddenly returned.
Now for the real struggle
As the striving for life begins.

POISON

Drink, sip, sin and jeer
Through the devil-eyed lens
Of drunken English beer.

Lures heart from path
Holds curse as light,
Hijacks the bogey tongue
With buggery and smite.

Binge, remove
Love, knowledge and care.
For rush, for lust
For history, for dare.

This soiree may commence anywhere,
The satanic push and pull of thoughts,
The morphing,

The tossing of the head.

Dry, dehydrated
Lost, decomposed.
A shake, a doze
A longing for change grows.

A longing to end the great soul eater,
To fend the toxic conductor,
To avoid the endless wind of day,
Toying with mind, work and play.

Drink, sip, sin and jeer
Through the devil eyed lens
Of drunken English beer.

MORNING STILLNESS

'*Morning stillness,* ' the iced island wept,
Behold Jack Frost's dawning claws!
Applauding Winter's disguise that somehow kept
Nature to defy man's laws.

Processes on hold, changes to keep
No platform to inform.
In the belly of this frozen plague
No orders keep men warm.

Ice on streets, Ice on eye
Ice on dreams and past.
Halt on present, halt on nigh
A season white in contrast.

What was fast is now taught speed
At limits slower than routine can take.
Inconvenienced and worried man will be,
Testing delicate patience to break.

ALCOHOLIC EMPATHY

When does one know they're in trouble
Which drink will it be that takes him over the edge
Which one will make him crack?
Which drink morphs him
From a mere, social laughing drinker
Into a possessed wretched creature.
Who creeks, sweats and smokes
And thinks about all the horrors in life.
All the shames endured and suffered.
All the morbid things, past, present and future.
All the wrongs, all the blackouts
All the inherited bits
And the cycles it creates.

It is no laughing matter.
It is a dreadful disease.
It is widespread

It affects some people on levels that it doesn't affect others.
Life experiences promote triggers.
It grows into a physical disease.
It develops a metabolism and glandular pattern,
It becomes a food, a stimulant, a peculiar friend.
Biology adapts.

So, don't forget the drink.
It's a boxing match
And you're always fighting.
The other fella is booze.
You evade him,
But one of these days if you're not careful
He's going to nail you right on the cheek
Down you go.
A continual fight, every day, week, month.
However frequent or infrequent
The ghost of the blackout
Will forever attempt to pounce.

For some, every day is a hurdle.
Then at bedtime, you put your head on the pillow and say
I've beaten that boxer again.
And so, you're stuck with that shadowy figure
Always coming at you
With every conceivable excuse
Take a drink.
I've got bad news, take a drink.

I've got good news, take a drink.
Without any exaggeration whatsoever
Denial and failure to get help could cost you a life.
My deepest sympathy to all affected
I pray you discover the tactics to step out of the devil's grip.

THE BALLAD OF LITTLE SAMMY

There's a little boy called Sammy,
Who plays skittles down my road,
He always seems so timid
When I walk by and say hello.

I saw him crying one day,
With bruises on his face,
Scars all down his backside,
Clutching a stolen money case.

I said:
"Where'd you find that?
It sure isn't yours,"
He said, *"I'm running from my papa,*
He makes me do these chores,
And when I stop,
He shouts, 'Sammy come here little boy!'
And when I hide,
He chases me with his fist.
And when he finds me,

He shouts Sammy you're in trouble,
And that's when he does the thing he does."

So, I asked him:
"Where are you going?"
He replied:
"To another land,
Far away from this demon,
As myself, I must be found.
I'm tired of being a punch-bag,
For a weary drunken thug,
I'm tired of falling over,
I'd fight back if I could.
Because when I stop,
He shouts, 'Sammy come here little boy!'
And when I hide,
He chases me with his fist,
And when he finds me,
He shouts Sammy you're in trouble,
And that's when he does the thing he does."

PICTURES IN PUBS

Resurrected calendars,
Toils of labour are now a trophy.
Pressures of time
Now gulped by rhyme.
Galleries of industry
Reclaiming lost lives.

Formed piece by piece
To be the piece it is now.
Broken to be whole.
Take these petals of dreams
Within your palm, eyes and soul,
Let the shadows aide your sips.

WONDERING

I was wondering
Why many lose sight of flowers and birds,
Too with colours, scents and thought.
Why barriers of fear are built
Then established within days,
Turning talent to dust.

I was wondering
Why a friend studied for twenty-six years,
To then struggle for work.
To be denied opportunity
And to be told,
One has wasted time.

I was wondering
What the world will be like for my grandchildren.
Will inheritance be stolen?
Will they be born into a dystopia?

Will they witness Armageddon?
Or will the years go by without harm.

I was wondering
Why we haven't learnt lessons
From malicious wars gone by.
Why we still pursue
The droughts of extremism,
And are tolerant when extremism pursues us.

I was wondering
Why men fight and die,
For tapestries of lies and dishonest governance.
Why trusted figures betray voters,
And why the voters
Persist in propping them up.

I was wondering
How tyrant warlords earn pay
And why civilian casualty is unaddressed.
Why morning news
Greets my day with a murder,
And how some political figures are not imprisoned for war crimes.

I was wondering
Why we ignore the world and her health.
How war is funded before the greenhouse.
Why millions continue to starve.
And when will our beloved Mother Nature

Finally grow sick of us.

I was wondering
If this poem speaks loudly to you,
If it is listened too
Or does it shoot into one ear.
Vacantly stir inside
And then exit via the other.

I was wondering
If these words will lead to change
Within your world and life.
Leading towards a road
More positive, worthwhile
Fulfilling and loving.

I was wondering
If the people that really need to read this
Will do so.
Or will global dominance be too busy
In continuing to write this poem,
Until one bastard is greedy enough
To write the final verse.

THE DEED OF RETIREMENT

Smoggy ancient mills
Aged cobble lanes,

Form a stark dictionary of pictures,
Of which the tides of muscle and memory meet.
And when they greet
In rare, enchanted accents
Beneath the spinning golden sun,
They chortle with joy
As the deed of retirement is done.

A dusted journal, a sterling pen
Grafters philosophy in class divine.
Explains day by day, line by line
Supressed emotion honestly defined.
As empires fall and crush a thousand men
There is no road to run.
Except to the cries of deceitful lies
As the deed of retirement is done.

In my pondering of age
Cruel weapons are hung,
Authority long swallowed
And jewels past down.
At last alone in gracious solitude
I take my final sip of rum.
And exhale nirvana,
As the deed of retirement is done.

Fini

Printed in Great Britain
by Amazon